Photography by Janet McNeil

WORKBOOK PRESS LLC

187 E Warm Springs Rd,
Suite B285, Las Vegas, NV 89119, USA

Website:https://workbookpress.com/
Hotline:1-888-818-4856
Email:admin@workbookpress.com

Ordering Information:
Quantity sales. Special discounts are available on quantity purchases by corporations, associations, and others.
For details, contact the publisher at the address above.

ISBN-13:   978-1-960752-32-1 (Paperback Version)
              978-1-960752-33-8 (Digital Version)

REV. DATE: 07/19/2023

SHAPED
with
PURPOSE

A Mosaic Collection of Inspirational Poetry and Short Stories

JANET MCNEIL

Contents

Acknowledgments

Rev. Dr. Charles Stanley, Pastor

"Adversity is one of God's effective tools to strengthen our faith."

Rev. Dr. Alyn E. Waller, Pastor

"And not only so, but we glory in tribulations also: knowing that tribulation worketh patience" Romans 5:3.

Rev. Dr. Herbert H. Lusk, II, Pastor

"The Lord came that we might have more abundantly, physically, spiritually, and eternally."

Joyce Meyer, Christian Speaker and Author of "The Power of Simple Prayer"

"We all need power in our lives, and prayer is the dynamic that releases His power, sometimes in dramatic ways."

Oswald Chambers, Author of "My Utmost for His Highest"

"Whenever God gives a vision to a saint, He puts him, as it were, in the shadow of His hand, and the saint must be still and listen."

Joel Osteen, Pastor, Televangelist, and Author

"Wake up every morning with a thankful attitude. Expect something good to happen in your life today."

Wayne Dyer, Motivational Speaker, and Author

"If you change the way you look at things, the things you look at change."

Janet McNeil

Introduction

Shaped with Purpose was written from spiritual enlightenment, in a poetic style, it exposes the secrets from the lens of my perspective.

At first, I was reluctant to publish the book, assuming that it would not be received in the light it was given. It required courage to overcome the fear of rejection, and bravely stand against potential opposition and criticism. I realize that my viewpoints are unique, and they are driven as a result of personal experiences. Even though, I pressed forward, standing on the strength of my faith, believing in God, and accepting His wisdom.

During this process, I experienced an epiphany in discovering there is power in words and envisioned how the book can be helpful to others. Several poems in the book concentrate on possibilities, positive thinking, and exercising the power of faith. The poetry was written fluently, guided with expressions to interlock the messages in a symphonic arrangement revealing the highs, lows, and enigmatic, and serving as a vital source of information.

It is a "Self-Help" approach that lends to an assortment of inspirational poems and non-fiction narratives created for interpretation and observation, intended to inspire, uplift, enlighten, and encourage. God's love is the divine source of all my inspiration, and it has shaped me with purpose.

"Happy is the man that findeth wisdom, and the man that getteth understanding." Proverbs 3:13 KJV

Janet McNeil

Dependence on You

No one to share my secrets
Not a person I can trust
I keep my feelings bottled inside
They're safe from being crushed

It's not easy to bear it alone
Not simple to talk with ease
Afraid to take a chance of betrayal
With one wearing hate on their sleeves

I hold back from sharing my story
In dread, it will be taken wrong
Somehow blame will get twisted
And turn on me another flaw

Depending on you is what matters
A stance I will always keep
All the hidden secrets within
Brought out from a well so deep

Uncovering knowledge of the world
A venture of sharing a devotion
I embrace it eagerly for change
I depend on you what is spoken

In a Quiet Heart

Christ says I can…

Believe…

When Christ entered my life, I believed and received Him as my personal Savior. My faith continues to grow, and by God's grace, progresses in His wisdom. Faith is the secret source of assurance, security, stability, and contentment in a world gone wild. Values and morals are fading in a society of tremendous hopelessness, introducing moods of emptiness. Living in a world sweltered in chaos and confusion intensifies, causing a great loss of moral values.

A source of help is within reach. As it is written in His word, God fulfills the needs of his people.

"And ye shall know the truth, and the truth shall make you free" (*King James Bible*) John 8:32.

Believe God's word and trust Him to guide you in His infinite wisdom. It will lead you to peacefulness, just as a child being nurtured to feel safe and protected in His Father's house.

The Father of Our Help

What do you do when you can't change things?
Who do you turn to for peace of mind?
Where is your comfort to live in peace?
Why continue to ignore the truth?

Our world is in turmoil
Not much we can change
We must adjust to it
Life's destiny we face

Uncertain days and times
A price paid by Jesus
We have the gift of life
His sacrifice to please us

God can no longer be ignored
Give Him the highest praise
It's time to call on Him for help
Divine protection always

God is in control we know
Some might concede others deny
Truth is seen remaining in time
Hearts can't find resolve why?

The message is we need help
More than the world can offer
Chaos, conflict, confusion, unrest
Unless we call on God our Father

Encouragement for Living Today

God's love gives purpose to what I do to encourage and inspire others. I have a desire to help the weak that have fallen into hopelessness and sadness. They are struggling to pick themselves up and are finding it difficult to stand again. I want to remain strong in my faith for it is the strength that I need for helping others find new hope to release the shackles holding them in bondage. God sheds new light on situations every day. We must believe. It is my desire wherever I go to allow this epiphany to bring encouragement to the hearts seeking a way out of difficult circumstances.

God works mysteriously through His word to encourage us to not live in the past. The past is gone and cannot be relived again. *"For lo, the winter is past, the rain is over and gone…"* Song of Solomon 2:11. When we look into the past, we see much of what has already affected us, which is symbolic of our history. History cannot be relived. Take a step and look forward to what the future may bring. In other words, "Live for today." Living for today gives us what we need to get through each moment, and take one moment at a time. We will find everything necessary to meet our specific needs and prepare us to reach for tomorrow's future.

We are reminded of our past thoughts, and the experience never goes away. But it is a memory. Reliving old experiences holds you like a prisoner being kept behind bars, and keeps you as a hostage, preventing progress from moving forward. Today is a new day, a new beginning, and a new time to live and embrace new beginnings. Time is of the essence to value the enjoyment of today. Consider a positive thought, create a new vision, or form a reason for living today.

(*King James Bible*) Isaiah 61:1

The Spirit of the Lord GOD is upon me; because the LORD hath anointed me to preach good tidings unto the meek; he hath sent me to bind up the brokenhearted, to proclaim liberty to the captives, and the opening of the prison to them that are bound.

Giving Assurance to Trust God

I am grateful to the Lord for assuring me that I can trust him.

For far too long I was unsure how to trust God completely. I relied on myself to take care of all of my problems. At least I thought I could. God showed me that someone will always be there to lean on and guide my steps. Now, I can get through adversities because I trust His word and offer praise.

I learned to trust God. He is true to His word. He picks me up when I fall, dries the tears from my eyes, cleanses all shame and hurt, watches me day after day keeping me safe in his loving arms, and all through the night protects me from harm and danger.

Listen to God's voice when he speaks. I was not convinced at first, but discovered through experience He is worthy. The day I relinquished my will through faith, justified in His word, I discovered the truth.

I encourage you to remain strong in your circumstances. God is omniscient; all-knowing. Learn of His power. Stand still in times of trouble because He will take care of you. He will not chasten you for your weaknesses but instead offer you comfort, love, and understanding through His miraculous power. Won't you trust him? I lean on Him on this unequivocally long journey called life. Time and patience are a part of the experience towards growth, knowledge, and understanding His way, and as a result, you will profit from His teachings.

Be willing. The test comes afterward. Yes, indeed it will be challenging to let go of yourself and surrender your will to God. Eventually, you will find it an honor to witness the birthing of miracles and abundant blessings He has in store for you. Unconditional love is freely imparted in the spirit. The rewards are not easily described here but be prepared with humble gratefulness when you receive them.

Keep the faith. God will see you through it all with power and victory through Jesus Christ. His plan will begin to shape your life.

Nurture your faith. Believe and honor Him daily. He has supreme power and authority to walk you through every circumstance along life's journey.

Trust God. Knowledge begins with God's Word. Through His promises rests the power of understanding.

*"Trust in the Lord with all thine heart; and lean not unto **thine** own understanding. In **all thy** ways acknowledge Him, and He shall direct **thy** paths"*

Proverbs 3:5-6.

God's Promise

He will bring you comfort
When you need Him there
With patience and confidence
Just call Him in prayer

He quietly knows your troubles
He shares your pain and cares
His loving Sovereign Grace
Comforts in your despair

Reflect on times you spend alone
Sustain as time passes by
When you say it is ok
Its faith in Him you rely

No person shapes this miracle
New hope for a brighter day
His will for you is promised
A gift of new life this way

The Master's work is beyond your thoughts
He gives an opportunity
In your petition to Him in prayer
In faith, you have the victory

When you're feeling down and low
And nothing seems fair to you
Reflect on His word in daily prayer
God's promise of endless truths

Verily, verily, I say unto you,
He that believeth on me hath everlasting life"
John 6:47

Spend Time with God

Have you taken a few minutes of your time to listen to God? Have you tried to forget about everything else going on in your life and spend quality time reading or listening to His word?

I am intrigued by reading and listening to God's Word. The Holy Bible is foremost the best reference book ever written. Great narrators represent written accounts of personal experiences of the Apostles and the extraordinary men and women lending to wisdom and spiritual nourishment. Men touched by the Holy Spirit illustrate in vivid imagery powerful visions of trials and tribulations, survival on the battlefield, imprisonment, sorrow, heartbreak, and loneliness. It depicts real-life stories revealing the self-evident truths that lay the groundwork for growing faith. Ultimately, it is a unique narrative of events leading to valuable principles for all readers.

The Bible records history's greatest authors, and the content might be difficult for some to grasp or discern, on the contrary for others it is understandable. It is an accessible guide of practical information and instruction for living and is a navigable passage, guarded with a specific purpose. It is a source of knowledge and wisdom to equip us with the courage and strength to confront life's adversities.

Life brings with it a world of troubles. There are failures and times of weeping. The Bible teaches us how to cope with matters of life, to be courageous and content, to be patient and keep the faith, and to love and depend on Jesus for help in times of need. There is a passage of reference in the Bible for everything. I recall many times of failures. I know we have a loving God who will always be there because He cares. *"Whosoever shall confess that Jesus is the Son of God, God dwelleth in him, and he in God"* 1 John 4:15. He ushers in peace where there is sorrow. His Spirit is so alive it shines brightly in my life, and it will do the same for you. His light of truth will guide you. A renewal of your spirit awaits you if you trust Him.

Come to Him with your troubles in prayer. Have a conversation with Him. He will talk with you in a secret place and wipe away your tears. God has never failed to fulfill a promise. Especially, the promise of unconditional love!

"For God so loved the world, that He gave His only begotten Son, that whosoever believeth in him should not perish, but have everlasting life." John 3:16.

Confusion and Fear

Once upon a time, people walked among each other without the snare of hatred. There was a time when peace defined unity, love defined respect, and human dignity defined character, the important qualities of leadership to raising children in the community, and teaching them in schools and at home.

Times have changed from the way it used to be. I see it happening more and more each day within the inner circles of friends and families. It appears that there is so much going on in today's society, too soon and too fast. There is rarely enough time to breathe. Most everyone is trying to get a piece of the pie, chasing the American Dream, oftentimes selfishly and greedily at whatever costs. Generally speaking, some are unable to appreciate the simple things of life anymore. Family households once sharing conversations at the dinner table are becoming practically obsolete.

Some children rarely play interactively outdoors. I would dare to say the average man or woman has little desire of owning a simple pair of shoes, dress, or slacks that are not popularly designed. Instead, the simpler lifestyle is replaced with high-priced designer items, computer tablets, cell phones, and fast food. Generally speaking, valued time once shared among family has been lost in the hustle and bustle of living. Children oftentimes act out when there is a need for love. They need Mommy and Daddy with them, close by, and less busy with their agendas. Yes, oftentimes parents are too busy for actual parenting to give children the attention they need. Devoting too much time gathering material things is not what's important in life compared to the needs of children, and should certainly not be the main focus. Furthermore, diamond watches, designer tags, fancy cars, fishing boats, or baggy pants and hood coverings only hide' the fear of failure, occupying space, or it is covering reality behind a mask of confusion.

Times have certainly changed in the greater sense for the worse. Darkness hides the light of human dignity that once shone in our communities. Presently, love and respect for one another are broken and insecure. In my opinion, a society that was once able to walk together is instead, running and hiding in confusion and fear.

Song of Joy

I awoke this particular morning with a thought in mind "Suffer little children to come unto me". I was so distraught thinking about the cares of life. Sorrow had taken over me. I could not understand why I'd been going through the same continuous struggles and dealing with them for most of my life. I tried to map out in my mind what I was going to do, and how I would handle this and that. Everything seemed so out of place. Distorted thinking, shuffling thoughts, and waddling in discouragement, I felt the urge to pray. I asked God to please bestow peace in my heart and soul, and give me strength to endure sorrow I felt, and instill knowledge of things I could not understand.

I prayed for peace and prosperity for my children and their families, traveling mercies, and special attention for the grandchildren with blessings of happiness in the difficult days to come. I prayed to God to provide a hedge of protection around me from my enemies and those that hate me.

A sigh of relief came over me soon after praying in a very peculiar way. At that moment, I felt grateful for being able to pray for others despite my problems. My worries and troubles seemed to slip away. Without another notion, I carried on with other matters of the day.

That afternoon I went to the kitchen, opened the refrigerator door and suddenly an amazing revelation emerged. Laughing out loud with excitement I said, "I understand!" I knew then that praying for others miraculously erased my sorrow. Somehow the overwhelming sadness I experienced in the morning turned into laughter that afternoon. It was clear God's divine intervention caused me to be joyful, and in the spirit of goodness, my worries disappeared. I was set free. The light of knowledge allowed me to see after all. Joy manifested so greatly and proved my prayers were heard. I praise him for giving me unspeakable joy to write this story, a "Song of Joy".

"O Lord my God, I cried unto thee, and thou hast healed me." Psalms 30:2

"Sing unto the Lord, O ye saints of his, and give thanks at the remembrance of his holiness" Psalms 30:4

"For his anger endureth but a moment; in his favor is life: **weeping** *may endure for a night, but joy cometh in the morning"* Psalms 30:5

Listen and Learn

Sometimes children have feelings of entitlement. This is not unusual because of who they are. Of course, they might think their parents should listen to them. Rightfully so, and we do, but they should also remember that as parents, we have already experienced many situations on the road of life, racked up quite a few experiences, and with good intentions, have a need to share these things for their good. These are reasons that they should listen as well. Wisdom is sometimes halted by stubbornness or selfishness, arrogance or ignorance; not used here as a negative connotation but for explaining its meaning; the lack of knowledge. Wisdom draws attention to the ability to make sensible decisions and judgments based on personal knowledge and experience.

As a parent, I know how important it is to listen. During my childhood, I spent countless occasions with the older generation, neighbors, and friends of the family. I absorbed a great deal of knowledge. I listened, watched, and learned. I continue keeping company with the elderly even in my adult years. I applied invaluable knowledge they willingly shared and use it as a guide. As a result, many choices I made were not perfect, but sensible. You don't have to be a rocket scientist to know that some circumstances are not foreseeable but a majority of them require a little "know-how." It keeps situations manageable. Gathering information, observation, listening, and reading along with experience are necessary elements in making good choices, and being informed helps this process.

Life throws many curb balls and some you might not see coming towards you. Wisdom can assist in this game. To begin with, you wouldn't want to wait until the pitcher throws the ball; instead, take your position on the plate and prepare for all angles it might come at you. This way you are prepared to receive what is coming not only for the hit but for the miss as well. In this scenario, you learn how to strategize, organize, and plan your position, and protect yourself mentally so that no matter how the ball is thrown, win or lose, you will be victorious. Listening is one of the most important elements of learning.

I have a responsibility to help others in the game of life which I've already played, and positioned to win because I listen.

Referring to the testimony of the Ancient Greeks (King James Bible). Those who teach best utter words out of their heart, that speak from an experience of spiritual and divine things. *"Behold, this is the joy of his way, and out of the earth shall others grow."* Job 8:19

Hidden Treasures

Whisper tenderly to everyone
The greatest gift is known by far
Softly spoken and rarely heard
Tells the world who we are
You must believe in yourself
Treasures are hiding inside
Dreams are real they do exist
Shake fear put pride aside
Your dreams will seem to shatter
Hold on you're almost there
Joy flows closer than ever
The power of love is shared
Keep the faith it is your strength
You don't have far to go
You'll discover heavenly love
That hails from skies above
Be true to what you believe
You're designed to be unique
Give love let gratitude show
Faith is yours to keep
Embrace precious time
With simple gifts we hold
Joy, love, truth, and more
Hidden treasures are yours

Guide Me

Guide me, merciful Father
Help me know what to do
I've been hurt and shamed by many
Mistreated and suffered too

Keep me close Dear Lord
All my hope is in you
I seek your guiding spirit
To lead me to your Will
Help me move the confusion
And have my mind set free
Lead me to your comfort Lord
Your truth my Source indeed
I turn no ways to man
For he has failed before
A heart of self-centeredness
With deaf ears, hears no more

To hear your voice enlightens me
Your word I do believe
That I might know the peace you bring
A guide of trust indeed
Reverence of amazing power
A vision is my plea
My mind is content Oh Lord
Thank you for guiding me

Let me Follow You

'Oh Lord each day I search your spirit to lead and guide me through

A guiding force of truth and kindness bears witness to you

Let me put myself aside and in everything give praise

Keep my vision and prayers for strength in all of my days

It's not easy running the race and without you, I can not

Neither dares to think I can without my source of help

When my mind is on edge fear creeps in and a miraculous

love from above

Erases my tears, eases my pain, and inspires me with love

Your kind of love is greatness, an awesome magnificence

Teach me Father what you Will, and let me follow you

Let me put myself aside in everything I do

Giving honor and praise my heart seeks one with you

With diligence, perseverance, and hope I am set free

Delight in serving your purpose is my prayer to thee

All I ask is eternal life, I do not deserve

Rejoicing in your word, a love you have reserved

Let me put myself aside, guided to surrender your way

And give all the glory and praise to you every day

Your kind of love is greatness, an awesome magnificence

Teach me Father what you Will, and let me follow you

The Rose Petal

The sweet smell of a rose petal
Sheds apart from the heart
At a glance a stillness of beauty
Curved layers set delicately apart
Eyes admire with delight
Through a glass of pleasant memories
Stored in a pane framed in love
Display cultivated varieties
A vast collection of joy to behold
Color pink, orange, red, and yellow
Exotically express around the globe
Serenely blush in a shadow
It leaves in my heart light for my soul
Mesmerizing alluring extravagance
A joyful moment a delightful bliss
Splendored rose petal magnificence

Re-Breathing to Silent Winds

Sweet silence from the movement of thought
Intrinsic peace abandons the wild
Shushed by air we feel as we breathe
Like melancholy, we're longing to hear
Re-breathing to silent winds
My energies depleted from these challenges
Some I meet every day
The world seems cruel by the nature of him
A dark, deep, evil within
Re-breathing to silent winds
Sorrow was born to hurt and pain
Paved destruction on the journey
Chaos and confusion sound the alarm
Selflessness is girdled
Re-breathing to silent winds
Silent silence calms my thoughts
Eagerly brings peace to darkness
Shush discomfort of the wild
Peace as we breathe in oneness
Re-breathing to silent winds

Living in the Struggle

It's not easy living day to day
Standing through everything that comes your way
You put up a fight to get some sleep
Tell folks to get off your back it's not that deep
You work hard with one thing on your mind
Feed your family and pay bills on time
A fight with the boss in a struggle to please
You can't do enough to put them at ease
Things break down you alone must fix
Nobody's around when you need them
You're tired and not well but that's not enough
You got to keep going no matter what
You keep it moving for a little dollar made
And try to make do with what you can
Friends are there but not too much
It takes up time to lend a hand
You sleep a little and work a lot
You just can't seem to get on top
Walking steadily the same every year
Now living in the struggle without a tear

Are you a Friend?

What defines a friend?

A friend will not insult you and never have regrets.

A friend will accept your character and accept your flaws with a smile.

A friend will make good use of the time shared to uplift, encourage, and sympathize

A friend will not talk negatively about you or invalidate you as a person.

A friend will show you ways of love and how it thrives in a relationship.

A friend will never abandon, neglect, or alienate you.

A friend will take time to call and see if you are living and well.

A friend will never leave you with tears of a broken heart.

Human emotions are like the delicate petals of a flower
When strong winds blow the petals eventually fall
The flower will never be the same again

When Blame is at the Door

Blame is at the door strangling me
Loosen the grip with a bit of kindness
No need to listen when ears are deafened
No need to speak winds hush each word
Take all I say for what it's worth
You'll find meaning inside my truth
No picking and pecking through the rubble
When genuineness already exists
It's not too much you can do or say
When words come across to blame
Take charge and get a new perspective
Too far-fetched when blind-sided
By whims of secrets, you only know
When it forces its way out as it does
Flying out of a mouth so freely
Unfairness begins to take hold
Let's say I take this into my care
Hold it my responsibility
I can't talk where there is no blame
Except when blame is at my door

Ignorance

Ignorance isn't just a cliché
The malady exists among men
A mind hindered by limitations
An ego faltered within
Ignorance is not easily known
A secret hidden in distress
Swarming in life unawares
Unknowing a consciousness exists
Unrecognized facts to realize
Too many don't understand
Have not a most valuable tool
To arch life's challenging demands
Interesting is an absent mind
An interior has little showing
Yet with pride and ignorance
Avoids the consequence of knowing

Building Life

You built me God into what I am from all I have been through
The secrets of my life exposed in praise I give to you
You whisper in my spirit to show me what to do
All the joy you gave to me the respect I give to you
Life is good because of you no matter what others think
Using any comparisons never truly equate
I see a deeper realm of worth and this I surely know
One that gives abundant life deep within my soul
Things cannot be measured by what you buy in life
Fine furnishings and flashy cars shining so bright
Life is reserved in humble faith and obedience to His will
His tempered spirit resides in those who choose and will stand still
Waiting requires patience beyond what you imagine
Time is measured in a manner whenever it will happen
It often takes a lifetime before God will speak to you
Listen carefully when it comes and you will know it too

Footprints

I don't know how long ago it happened. It caught me by surprise and stopped me in my tracks. I looked back and Footprints changed my direction.

I was drawn to a place where beautiful art was displayed. For hours I explored each piece trying to find something to take with me, and anything wouldn't do. I looked around but nothing appealed to me. I probably should have given up because nothing caught my eye but I continued looking.

Time was passing by as I kept watch. And then, strangely an eye-catching piece of artwork appeared. I realized immediately that it was a divine choice made for me. The painting spoke to my heart. The message was clear that I would take it home with me. It was mine to own. A painting of Jesus' love is displayed for everyone to see.

~ I am comforted each time I gaze upon the magnificent artwork symbolizing His divine love ~

"No man hath seen God at any time. If we love one another, God dwelleth in us, and His love is perfected in us" 1 John 4:12.

Wisdom Approaches

Wisdom approaches hide not thyself
To show how things should be
A story told some years ago
Before our eyes could see
Countless acts of selfishness
War and conflict soar
Blinded eyes and cruelty
As history unfolds
Confronting challenges long ago
Shame loose and harbored fears
A pendulum of competing foes
Beneath dark tombs shed tears
Purge selfishness brings forth good
Cry out and let it be known
Surely repress the purest nature
As the beginning of time has shown
Renew the spirit breathe new wisdom
An aroma to nourish the mind
Freely given to all drawn near
Blown from the nostrils of time
Climb with courage you must move on
Strife reckoned in the race
Resistance is a price to pay
Victory shows its face
Unveiling itself surprisingly
The meaningful assurance this way
A clear vision of evidence past
Charred mysteries assembled of clay

Untouchable Gems

As we travel the road of life, sometimes we encounter entanglements or circumstances that prevent us from reaching our true destiny of happiness. Constantly challenged with bad situations for instance, job loss, homelessness, dysfunctional family relations, or having to come face to face with mean people who would rather see us fail than succeed – things like that.

Stones were thrown to and fro, we catch some and miss a few. If we only stop for a moment and realize the value of the "untouchable gems" we have in our possession. Gems are precious jewels cut and polished for our use. We have ownership of them as a privilege of choice. As we walk and talk, smile and laugh, nevertheless, we still have the opportunity to focus on what will be beneficial to retain good posture amid bad situations. Oftentimes, our natural tendencies cause us to lose grip of our senses to listen, forgive, show compassion, or be patient. Unknowingly, these are the attributes at the center of the gem. No matter what circumstances we face, a positive mind will generate positive energies like a gemstone emanating radiant light.

Of course, while in the hustle and bustle of life, there will be times we will be pushed to our limits. Our patience runs short in a fast-moving, fast-forward-driven society stressed by the limitations of time as we strive to reach our goals on the beaten path to find happiness. During these times we rarely focus on the little things or notice real values of importance. We should err to caution and not take it for granted. We have the privilege of choice.

Kindness, selflessness, compassion, patience, and above all love for one another is God's way of gifting us with valuable gems for our travels. Be encouraged, but more importantly, concentrate on the virtuous attributes that will surely elevate the experience.

Gems of life are given with a purpose

The stones were thrown to and fro

Catching some, and missing few

Untouchable gems will show

Life holds valuable privileges

To speak, to laugh, to breathe

So cherish the gems that you possess

Store safe in your heart and keep

Life brings reflections of images

Values unnoticed drift away

A touch, a smile, a sense of the wind

Assembled in potter's clay

Tread the rugged road of life

Some paths you wish to forget

Close your eyes and concentrate

Untouchable gems are your safety net

In the Spirit

"I can do nothing without God"

I reached a point in my life knowing that I am unable to conjure enough thoughts or strategies to solve my problems alone. I need the power of the Holy Spirit to guide me as I travel on this path called life.

I rely on the Heavenly Father to help me through my situations, especially those that are beyond my control. With patience and faith, I can endure the wait and follow His direction. Faith and patience produce strength. Whether I need guidance for a decision I need to make or have to take a specific action concerning business, change or start a new career, seek new relationships, or whatever it may be; He is the appointed safety guide.

Many years ago, I accepted the Lord Jesus Christ as my personal Savior. His spirit dwells in my heart. It was a miracle to find a new source of freedom. On many occasions, I cried out and no one heard me, except Him. I began to read the Bible, study its interpretations with Bible-based literature, and listen to sermons and various speakers. A scripture I favor is as follows:

"Delight thyself in the Lord, and He will give thee the desires of thine heart", Psalms 37:4 KJV

As I shuffle through many complex situations over wide plains as far as the eyes can see and valleys low. I can press on under His direction compassing the way. He is the pilot of the circumstances I encounter; always steady on course perfectly steering a way out. I live confidently in His love. He is gracious, merciful, and faithful.

It isn't always easy to explain my thoughts, how I see things, or what I know and how I came to know it. I understand. However, when expressions are complex for the natural mind; incomprehensible of man's understanding, it is a far greater knowledge reaching further in the realm of supernatural wisdom. That phenomenon can only be experienced. Glory to God!

Revelation 3:20 KJV

*"Behold, I stand **at the door**, and **knock**: if any man hears my voice, and **opens the door;** I will come into him and will sup with him, and he with me."*

Teach Love

It is difficult to teach the value of love when you have been hurt again and again by the fiery darts of life. But for those of you who are hurting, remember in this message, you are not alone. In a deeper realm of my perspective, I realize the impact of each spurt of pain you feel can be felt around the world. Some are very sick and unable to feel good anymore. Some feel the effects of loneliness, choosing to endure the pain alone, giving up, and giving in. Many people are dying from a deep depression in a world that appears to have forgotten them, unsheltered of undulating motion in a sea of sadness, in the absence of vitality to hope, drowns in despair and hopelessness.

Let this message reassure you there is an alternative direction you can follow aimed at restoring optimism, comfort, and freedom in your life.

Love is the answer.

Love is a direct manifestation of God dwelling inside of you. It means you have ownership of love. There are so many people unaware of how to access the power of love and use this precious gift God freely granted you. We all need it in our lives and to use it for the advantage of others. Help others by spreading love. If you take a moment and think about it, how will anyone cope with countless sufferings life springs on us like disappointments, blame, hate, discouragements, sorrow, guilt, and death? Void of love, it is impossible to thrive in a healthy climate of positive mind and forgiveness. There is no better alternative than love. God is love. It is the greatest power to draw the strength you need in any circumstance. Understanding the spirit of love and how it comes into being is forgiveness. It remedies painful and hurtful situations, heals the heart and mends the mind, and eventually sets you free from the anguish you might feel. Forgive yourself, forgive others, and ask God for His forgiveness. Our sovereign Father loves us so much. He allows divine love to enter the heart of every man and woman if you receive it. The power of love will give you the courage to forgive others.

If you read this message, it is a testimony your spirit is alive, generated, and motivated. And the emotions you feel right now come directly from the spirit within you. Love lives inside of you, so take ownership of it. It is not because of what you have done in your life but because of who you are, a child of God. God love you unconditionally since the beginning of time and granted us all the wonderful gift of love. Why not use it?

Reach Out to Him

Reach out to Him for all your needs; He's always there for you

Don't be afraid to trust in him, He wants to see you through

The pain and sorrow and all your fears are needless to bare

When life deceives, we believe and learn that it's not there

At times we think about life's happiness and things we hold so dear

A laugh, a smile, a memory too it soon will disappear

A moment kind of happiness doesn't last too long

Until we reach out to Him, we'll understand this song

A sweet and precious kind of love he lends a helping hand

And helps us see the good in us and soon we'll understand

We're faultless by the blood He shed Atonement for our sins

No more to bear the guilt and shame with love and care in Him

Reach out to Him for all your needs he's always there for you

Don't be afraid to trust in him he wants to see you through

Our Salvation in Jesus Christ

God is our redeeming power gifted and justified in His word. It asserts the torturous crucifixion of Jesus Christ on the cross at Calvary for our sins, and the miracle of His resurrection proclaiming He is the son of God. The New Testament of the Bible holds amazing powers accentuating over and over again, marvelous truths and revelations as a means to re-establish the dynamic need for His people to bear witness to the Gospel of Jesus Christ.

And my speech and my preaching were not with enticing words of man's wisdom, but in demonstration of the Spirit and of power:" *1 Cor. 2:4*

Even when things look grave

God will bring you peace

He lends a shoulder to lean on

In tough times and unhappiness

He allows for things you need

Contentment remains in the heart

Steadfast in hope of HIS promise

He fulfills the broken heart

A spirit so pure and comforting

He puts your troubles at rest

Seek Him for your help always

Sustained in love you're blessed

God is sovereign with love and tender mercies and amazing power. *"But that ye may know that the Son of man hath power on earth to forgive sins" Matthew 9:6.*

To achieve salvation from the bondage of the past broken, deliverance is breathed into God's children. Only God has the power justified by faith and deliverance accomplished in Jesus Christ.

"And they were astonished at his doctrine: for His word was with power" Luke 4:32

"Salvation is for everyone who believes and the needs of ordinary people are fulfilled. There is never a demand for intellect or unusual spiritual endowments. We respond and receive what God has done for us as Paul the apostle suggests we say, "Yes" to his great Amen"

"For all the promises of God in him are yea, and in him Amen, unto the Glory of God by us." 2 Cor. 1:20

"The righteousness of God is revealed to those who bring to its reception, the necessary quality of faith – a divine nature that cannot be purchased, but can only be received by faith. Wait in humble trust for what God is willing to give and then receive it with gratitude and without pride. This is what Paul calls faith" (The Interpreter's Bible vol. IX)

"For therein is the righteousness of God revealed from faith to faith: it is written, the just shall live by faith." Romans 1:17

The Richness of Gold

People scatter about I'm proud
Hard to describe right now
Seeing pictures of many faces
Under a heart of gold
Gold is priceless
Many cannot afford
Not plated on chrome
But genuinely earthed and pure
A precious rare commodity
Only a few perfect the mind
Kindly spoken to ears have shown
Emotions emoting inside
Never heard her crying
Always strong, self-governing
Dignity and confidence
Unwittingly divulge belongings
People sharing gentleness
Compassion shows how much
Giving, listening, sharing, and caring
Together with time and trust
Surpassing stress and anxiety
Fought all doubts and fears
Let go of absolute dependency
Brought love I need to hear
I have a new vision of people now
Colored on a canvassed sky
Imparting pleasant impressions
Prove rarity now realized
Love is one to another
And not plated on chrome
A genuine kind and priceless gem
Behold a heart of gold

Restoration

I trample through muddy waters
Each step like iron and steel
A heavy load I carry for miles
Searching for comfort I kneel
Through foggy nights in darkness
Steady forging to these heights
Anchors weighing down on me
Move motionless all night
I seek refuge from a powerful influence
Sweet victory from these trials
And though I never gave up
A journey to a place I found
Crossing this road is impossible
Without Father by my side
As He sits quietly, smiling and says
Keep working my sweet child
Know I am by your side you see
You'll never know what happens next
I've known you since you were a baby
Still cuddling with love to help
You've been through so many trials
I know because I saw you through
When all seemed so impossible
Faith and trust lead to truth
You toughed it out when others hurt you
Uncountable ways past one
They're still trying to make you fail
What I've seen makes me shun

I admire your strength never give up
Striving to live and help others
Denying yourself so others might have
For I give you the grace of wonder
My child whose heart has been broken
You have my gifts of love
Joy, happiness, and blessings restored
Deserving of care from above

My Wings

I am spreading my wings hoping to find everything I have reached for and being resilient to discover what lies ahead.

I stretch my wings, lift my head, open my eyes, and smile. I am flying to places I have never been, delighting in the experience that will not manifest itself as a dream. I am spreading my wings as tomorrow is not promised, so I am spreading my wings today.

About the Author

Janet McNeil is a native of Philadelphia, PA. She married at a young age and cared for her family. She recognizes her life experiences are God's blessings, for which she is grateful.

Her achievements are diverse in work and study. The areas include Health Technology, Education, Communications, and Administration, to name a few. She has an Associate in Medical Laboratory Sciences. She also earned an Associate Degree in Communication in Speech and an Academic Certificate in Leadership Studies that she acquired through a dual degree program. The courses of her studies include Elementary Education, Statistics, Psychology, Philosophy, Public speaking, Community Theory, and Creative Writing. She worked in the public school system and is a mentor for the at-risk adult population in the community. She recently received a Bachelor's Degree in Communication.

Janet became an author several years ago and she also sings professionally. She has devoted her life to her responsibilities of giving, caring for, and serving her family, Churches, Schools, Hospitals, and Communities.

She is a virtuous woman, morally and spiritually grounded, and worships God. She is artistic with an innate passion to nurture souls with care and compassion with an artistic freedom that abounds from the love of God. *"For by grace are ye saved through faith; and that not of yourselves: it is the gift of God."* Ephesians 2:8.

www.ingramcontent.com/pod-product-compliance
Lightning Source LLC
Chambersburg PA
CBHW040849120626
46547CB00001B/87